BASEBALL
IN
DENVER

Robert "Bus" Campbell was a renowned expert in understanding proper pitching mechanics. He also had a keen ability to convey that knowledge to many decades worth of big-league baseball players hailing from the state of Colorado; some are still enjoying big-league careers to this day. Bus lived in Littleton, just south of Denver, but was a graduate of Denver's Manuel High School with famed big leaguer Bruno Konopka. Bus worked with Little Leaguers to Cy Young–award winners and members of the National Hall of Fame. He is credited with tutoring Roy Halladay since adolescence and signing him to his first professional contract while a scout with the Toronto Blue Jays. Bus also helped resurrect Jaime Moyer's career in the early 1990s. He tutored over 30 current or former big-league pitchers, including Goose Gossage, Steve Busby, Shawn Chacon, Jesse Crain, Scott Elarton, Cal Eldred, Nate Field, Luke French, Burt Hooten, Steve Howe, Danny Jackson, Mark Knudsen, Mark Langston, Brad Lidge, and Clint Zavares. This list leaves out countless others who made it to the professional ranks. Bus never accepted a dime for all of his time and tutelage. He served as pitching coach at South and Littleton High Schools, University of Colorado, the fabled Boulder Collegians, University of Northern Colorado, University of Denver, University of Iowa, and lastly at Heritage High School before his passing in the spring of 2008. Bus scouted for the Cardinals, Royals, Reds, Angels, Blue Jays, and Milwaukee Braves of Major League Baseball. Inducted into the Colorado Sports Hall of Fame in 1987, Bus was the consummate family man who was incredibly endearing to all who knew him. His impact on the game of baseball has been immense.

FRONT COVER: Babe Ruth takes batting practice at Merchants Field in October 1927, while in the background Lou Gehrig signs autographs.

COVER BACKGROUND: Bears Stadium is seen on Opening Day in 1948.

BACK COVER: Shown in this 1886 photograph are the Denvers, the city's first truly organized baseball club.

BASEBALL
IN
DENVER

Matthew Kasper Repplinger II

ARCADIA
PUBLISHING

Published by Arcadia Publishing
Charleston, South Carolina

Library of Congress Control Number: 2013935600

For all general information, please contact Arcadia Publishing:
Telephone 843-853-2070
Fax 843-853-0044
E-mail sales@arcadiapublishing.com
For customer service and orders:
Toll-Free 1-888-313-2665

Visit us on the Internet at www.arcadiapublishing.com

To my family, who taught me that we are all family;
thankfully, I was raised in a baseball family.

CONTENTS

ACKNOWLEDGMENTS

I would like to acknowledge Jay and Alice Sanford, as they were so incredibly gracious and generous with their time. Jay, thank you especially for your immense knowledge of all things Denver and baseball and for being such a warm and loving person. It was a pleasure working with you.

Thanks also go to my baseball friends: Eric Absher, Paul Parker, Gino Grasso, Chris Campassi, Trent Kutler, Matthew Jerebker, Roland Hemond, John Thorn, Rob Neyer, Jonah Keri, Maury Wills, Marc Johnson, Bob Burris, Irv Brown, Cory Schwartz, Meredith Wills, Sabra Anknar, coach Gary Bishop, and Bus Campbell.

Unless otherwise noted, *Baseball in Denver* photographs are from Jay Sanford's collection.

INTRODUCTION

Prior to the arrival of major-league baseball in the Mile High City, many Americans thought of Denver, Colorado, as a beautiful town with a view of the Rocky Mountains that other cities would die for. Others thought of Denver as the gateway to Ski Country USA and as the home of the Broncos and John Elway.

In 1991, when Major League Baseball awarded Denver a National League expansion franchise, many in the baseball world were doubtful that Denver could become a baseball town. But the city's faithful were not surprised when, in its inaugural season in 1993, the Colorado Rockies set a single-season attendance record. Those not familiar with Denver's sports history would be surprised to know that the city has always been a baseball town.

With Denver still in its infancy and the Civil War entering its second year, the first recorded game of "base ball" (in the spelling of the time) in Denver took place on April 26, 1862. The "McNeils Side" defeated the "Hulls Side" 20-7. The city of Denver grew rapidly, and the amateur game spread quickly as well. Neighborhoods and merchants established teams and issued challenges, through newspapers, for games on Sunday afternoons. As demand grew for more and more baseball, the competition for talented players became intense, and the practice of paying individual players became commonplace. In Denver and throughout Colorado, the level of play had developed to the point that the *St. Louis Globe-Democrat* began to cover the region's games in 1876. The influx of professional players into Denver allowed team owners to begin charging spectators to see their clubs play. In 1879, the Denver Browns became the first fully professional team when it represented the city in a series of games against a Salt Lake City ball club.

In 1886, a team named simply the Denvers became the city's first participant in organized baseball when it joined the new Western League. The club boasted seven men who would go on to the big leagues, including Joe Straub, Dan Dugdale, Billy Mountjoy, Baldy Silch, George Tebeau, and "Flaming" Darby O'Brien. The arrival of Dave Rowe and George Tebeau in Denver was vital to the expansion of professional and amateur baseball in the city in the 1880s. Rowe and Tebeau are rightly referred to as the "fathers of Denver baseball." At various times, both men played major-league baseball, managed at the professional level, and owned the Denver minor-league franchise.

Major-league teams regularly barnstormed through Denver, starting when Dave Rowe brought his Kansas City Cowboys to town in 1886. Next came the Philadelphia Phillies (1887), the Chicago White Stockings (now the Cubs), and the All-America Team, which had embarked on a world tour in 1888. The St. Louis, Cleveland, and Boston teams also played in Denver in the 1880s. Denver had developed into such a hotbed for baseball that George Tebeau was able to convince the renowned Cap Anson to bring his Chicago team to the city in 1891 for spring training. Tebeau also championed the inclusion of African American professional players, such as George Taylor and William Castone, on the rosters of white teams.

Denver baseball fans knew talent when they saw it, and they saw an abundance of it. Before the dawn of the 20th century, nearly 20 of the city's players reached the major leagues. When the Colorado Rockies took the field at Mile High Stadium on April 9, 1993, in front of over 80,000 fans, Denver became a big-league town—but Denver had always been a baseball town. Dave Rowe and George Tebeau would have been proud.

—Jay Sanford

1

P I O N E E R S A N D P L A C E S

The Broadway Grounds were located at Broadway Boulevard and Colfax Avenue between Sixteenth Street and Lincoln Avenue. This photograph was taken from the Colorado State Capitol Building, looking north-northwest. The domed building in the center is the Arapahoe County Courthouse, located on the future sight of the May D&F Store and the famous ice rink and clock tower. The Broadway Grounds site was used for baseball in Denver as early as 1862.

McPHEE, 2d B., Cincinnatis

OLD JUDGE
CIGARETTE FACTORY
GOODWIN & CO., New York.

For 18 years, John "Bid" McPhee was the preeminent second baseman on the preeminent professional baseball team, the Cincinnati Reds. His inclusion in the National Baseball Hall of Fame, albeit only recent (2000), was just a matter of time. Bid was the last second baseman to play the position without a glove. This fact is all the more impressive, as he was so highly touted for his impeccable defensive skill. McPhee was notable for several reasons, including his status as Denver's first big-league baseball player and the first National Baseball Hall of Fame member to hail from Denver. The official historian of Major League Baseball, John Thorn, can be credited for championing McPhee's induction into the hall.

The T.S. Clayton Baseball Club of Denver poses for a team portrait around 1888. Shown are, from left to right, (first row) Caplinger (P) and Mulqueen (C); (second row) Graham (CF), Smith (3B), Foulkes (MGR), Watt (RF), and Shackelford (2B); (third row) Ganser (C), Trease (1B), Holzman (SS), and Hegel (LF). Clayton was a hatmaker whose shop was located at 1121 and 1123 Fifteenth Street in Denver. He also served as Denver's fire chief for a time around the turn of the century.

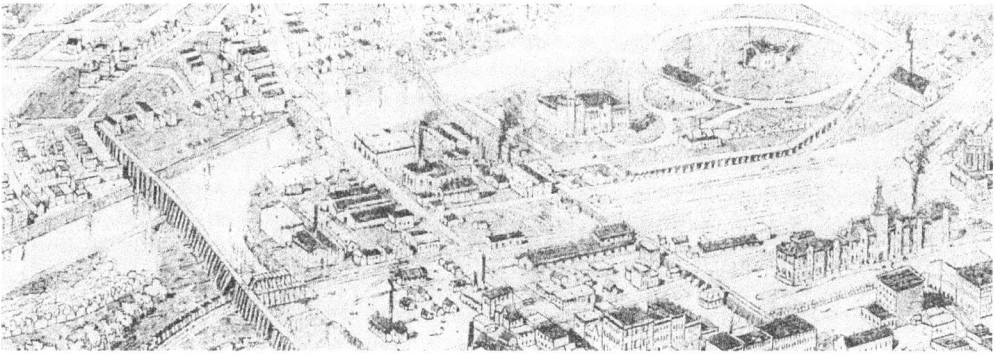

For a number of years, Riverfront Park (above) was the most prominent baseball field in the Denver area. Nationally known publisher and Denver resident John Brisben Walker (right), who founded the magazine *Cosmopolitan*, owned the land and is credited with erecting the grandstand, which at the time rivaled most other ballparks. The facility was used not only for baseball but also served as a horse track, a velodrome, and the circus grounds. Riverfront Park was located just west of Union Station, between Sixteenth and Twentieth Streets, and was bordered on the northwest by the Platte River.

Charles Leichsenring was a German immigrant who arrived in Denver in 1863 and quickly became successful as a saloon and restaurant owner in the area of Sixteenth and Market Streets. Leichsenring, with his sons Edward and Clarence, was involved in bringing professional baseball to Denver in the 1880s. George Tebeau, one of the "fathers of Colorado baseball," was Leichsenring's son-in-law. In this photograph, Leichsenring is wearing medals he received from England's Queen Victoria after rescuing British sailors from drowning in the Mississippi River.

In 1886, the Denvers became the Mile High City's first organized baseball team. That same year, they won the Western League's first pennant. Denver's uniforms were "old gold," with a secondary color of red for lettering, stockings, belts, and the striped caps. Among the players shown are Flaming Darby O'Brien, Jack Ryan, Baldy Silch, and George "White Wings" Tebeau.

Larimer Street Park sat on the edge of a quickly growing metropolis, but getting there was made simple by means of the Larimer Street horse-car trolley. One could take the trolley directly to the gate of the ballpark at Thirty-second and Larimer Streets.

David Rowe was a major-league player and manager who played sporadically in Denver as early as 1883 and as late as 1889. At various times, he owned baseball franchises in Denver, Omaha, and Des Moines. He was the first big-league ballplayer to make Denver his offseason home and has been credited for bringing the first big-league teams to Denver in the 1880s.

ROWE, Mg'r, Denvers
OLD JUDGE
CIGARETTE FACTORY.
GOODWIN & CO., New York.

George Tebeau (December 26, 1861–February 4, 1923) had two nicknames over the course of his life in baseball. He was known as "White Wings" because of his excellent grace and speed and his well-dressed appearance. More significantly, he was later given the nickname the "father of Colorado baseball," and for good reason. He was a star player on Denver's first organized team, the Denvers. Tebeau played professionally for Cincinnati, Cleveland, and Washington. He founded the American Association, managed the Denver Bears, and owned franchises in Denver, Kansas City, and Louisville. He also helped found the American League with friend and sportswriter Ban Johnson.

ED HANLON'S GREAT CATCH AT DENVER.

This is an artist's depiction of Ed Hanlon's great catch at Riverfront Park during one of the big-league barnstorming trips made from 1886 through the early 1890s. The Kansas City Cowboys in 1886, Philadelphia Phillies in 1887, and Chicago White Stockings all played at Riverfront Park. Another touring team that came to Denver was the All-American Team, part of the Spalding Australian Tour, in 1888.

The original Broadway Park was as deep as any ballpark; only Dave Rowe was known to have hit a home run over the wall, over 400 feet away. The first Broadway Park burned down, and a new grandstand and auxiliary seating were constructed, but the original field location remained. In 1891, Cap Anson's Chicago White Stockings participated in spring-training games each afternoon versus George Tebeau's Denvers.

John "Bud" Fowler was a 19th-century African American baseball pioneer. He joined the Pueblo Pastimes in 1885 and opened the door for other professional black players in Colorado, such as George Taylor and William Castone. Between the 1885 and 1886 seasons, Fowler gained further notoriety by performing in vaudeville plays. For a time, he was so successful in this pursuit that he owned his own playhouse near Fifteenth and Champa Streets.

John W. Jackson, or "Bud Fowler," as he was known to the baseball world, was the first African American baseball player by several years. He played the longest (10 seasons) of any of the more than 70 black players in what was considered a minor league from 1877 (the beginning of minor-league professional baseball) through the end of the 19th century, when black players were effectively barred from white teams. The first documented mention of Fowler as a player is in April 1878, when he pitched for the Chelsea team in Massachusetts. On April 24 of that year, he pitched in an exhibition game and was victorious over the Boston Nationals of George Wright and James O'Rourke fame.

Joe Tinker (July 27, 1880–July 27, 1948) was a major-leaguer, most famously with the Chicago Cubs teams that created a dynasty between 1906 and 1910, winning the National League pennant each of those years. Tinker was elected to the National Baseball Hall of Fame in 1946. George Tebeau can be credited with discovering the future great. Tinker was the Denver Bears shortstop at the age of 19 but, for reasons unknown, was released on June 9, 1900. He was picked up by Butte in the Montana State League before moving on to the Chicago Cubs in the National League. He is famously mentioned in the well-known poem "Baseball's Sad Lexicon" by Franklin Pierce Adams: "The saddest words I ever heard were Tinker to Evers to Chance."

ROCKY MOUNTAIN NEWS

DENVER, COLORADO.   WEDNESDAY, JUNE 6, 1888   PRICE, FIV

RIVER FRONT PARK

Sixteenth St. Three Minutes Drive from Tabor Blk.

PHILIP McCOURT, Manager.

Seating capacity after June 14, Seven Thousand. Can be engaged for desirable entertainments.

Concerts,
Political Meetings,
School Exhibitions,
Races Half-mile Track,
Base Ball, Picnics, etc.

Enclosed Stage for Light Opera and Concerts 70 feet by 10 feet

Street cars run directly to entrance gate; fare five cents.

Exposition Building dancing floor; seats fifteen hundred.

Training Stables with privilege of track; $5 per month; artesian water

OFFICE, 2215 FIFTEENTH STREET

This Riverfront Park advertisement ran in the *Rocky Mountain News* on Wednesday, June 6, 1888.

"Big Bill" Everitt was a hard-hitting infielder (1B/3B) who played in the 1890s for the Chicago White Stockings, which later became the Cubs. Everitt was given the difficult task of replacing Cap Anson but did so adequately, as he was often one of the league's leading hitters.

Willie "Bill" Hogg was a splendid specimen of an athlete. He stood six feet in his stockings and weighed 200 pounds. A right-handed pitcher, he commanded the respect of opposing players. He was a "heady" pitcher and a hard man to outguess. Hogg understood baseball from every angle and used it to his advantage in his delivery to the plate. Sadly, his playing career was cut short due to tuberculosis, which he picked up while playing in New Orleans. He passed away in December 1909 at the age of 28.

Henry Schmidt was a pitcher for the Denver Bears. He might have been a good foil for Christy Mathewson, but he declined the opportunity. Schmidt was originally from Texas, but he spent much of his adult life in Denver. On opening day at the Polo Grounds in 1903, Schmidt started for Brooklyn and Mathewson for New York. It was Schmidt's very first major-league appearance. Astonishingly, he prevailed 9-7, and as the season progressed he pitched three consecutive shutouts and won 22 games. The following winter, Brooklyn owner Charles Ebbets sent his young star a contract for 1904. It came back unsigned, with a brief note attached: "I do not like living in the East," Schmidt wrote, "and will not report." He never appeared in the majors again.

BURT E. JONES, Pitcher,
ST. LOUIS, 1900.

Burt "Cowboy" Jones (1874–1958), who pitched for the first St. Louis Cardinals, hailed from Golden, where he was a graduate of the Colorado School of Mines. He later became the school's head baseball coach and then athletic director. A teammate of Hall of Famers Cy Young and Jesse Burkett, Jones played baseball in the Colorado State League and semipro baseball during the 1890s in Denver and Pueblo. He pitched for the Colorado Springs Millionaires from 1902 to 1904. Former Denver player Patsy Tebeau was his manager with Cleveland and St. Louis. Cowboy Jones was wonderfully popular in Golden, later serving as mayor for a time and as sheriff of Jefferson County. He is buried in the Golden Cemetery.

Roy Allen Hartzell (July 6, 1881–November 6, 1961) played major-league baseball from 1906 to 1916. He started his career with the St. Louis Browns (now the Baltimore Orioles) and was later traded to the New York Highlanders (now the Yankees), where he finished his career. Hartzell was a native of Golden and participated in the first game played at Fenway Park in 1912, credited with the first RBI there. He is buried in the Golden Cemetery.

Howard Ellsworth "Smoky Joe" Wood (October 25, 1889–July 27, 1985) spent 14 seasons in the majors. He played for the Boston Red Sox from 1908 to 1915, where he was primarily a pitcher, and for the Cleveland Indians from 1917 to 1922, mostly as an outfielder. He is among only 13 pitchers since 1900 to have won 30 or more games in one season (going 34-5 in 1912). George Tebeau to a certain degree can be credited with discovering Smokey Joe Wood prior to his catching on with Kansas City, with whom he debuted. Wood was also known to have played on a bloomers team while still in the amateur ranks.

David L. Foutz moved to Denver from Maryland as a teenager. He played for Colorado's first professional team, the 1879 Denver Brown Stockings. He was seen again playing for the 1880 Denver Queen City's and also caught on with the 1882 Leadville Blues, winning 39 of 40 games that season as his team won the Colorado state title. In 1883, Foutz was pitching for the Bay City Club of the North Western League, and during that season and the next he earned such a reputation as a pitcher that in order to secure his services, the St. Louis club of the American Association had to purchase the entire Bay City club. Brooklyn struggled to obtain his rights from St. Louis but did so in 1888, which proved fortuitous as the team won the National League championship in 1890. Foutz's brother was the mayor of Leadville.

E.A. Willoughby was the winning pitcher in the first organized baseball game played in Denver, in April 1862. The McNeils defeated the Hulls 20-7.

Henry M. Porter, who also played in that first game in 1862, went on to found Porter Hospital and was a prominent figure in the state of Colorado.

The Denver Athletic Club baseball team of 1892–1893 poses for a portrait. Players shown here include Hannington (C), Fields (OF), Turner (P), Pfouts (OF), McCracken (SS), Bowen (OF), O'Brian (3B), Kassler (2B), Trease (1B), Whitney (P), Burbee (OF), and Willoughby (INF). Turner and Whitney are the players holding the baseballs.

The Northwestern University players in this 1877 photograph are William Gray Evans (P), Martin Robinson (SS), Edward Kinman (2B), William Hamilton (3B), Clarence Gardner (OF), Frank Knappen (OF), Edward Adams (OF), ? Smith (1B), and ? Yott (C). This team lost to the Chicago White Stockings 13-5. Evans eventually became president of the Denver Tramway Company. His father, John Evans, was the second territorial governor of Colorado who had a mountain (Mount Evans) and a city (Evanston, Illinois) named after him.

The 25th Infantry Regiment marches at Fort Logan in Denver in October 1898. This particular unit had an outstanding baseball team from 1894 to 1919. From this unit came the core of what was to become the 1920 Kansas City Monarchs in the first year of the Negro League.

The 25th Infantry team at Fort Logan in Denver poses in 1899. The African American players include Cpl. William Crawford, Sgt. A. Reid, Sergeant Daniels, Pvt. S. Gardner, Private Fullbright, Private Carter, and Pvt. Avery Craig. The white players include: Lt. R.J. Burt, Lieutenant Hunt, Lt. William T. Schenck, and Lieutenant McNally. In December 1899, Bill Crawford died following a game in the Philippines between the 25th Infantry and the 41st Volunteers. A small bolo knife hanging from his belt entered his abdomen as he slid back to second base on an attempted pickoff play. On January 29, 1900, William Schenck also died in the Philippines Islands; he was shot while leading his detachment of scouts through the "Subig Cut" between Subig and Castillejos. This photograph shows a truly historic team largely ahead of its time, being the first recorded military team to have blacks and whites playing on the same side.

These c. 1913 photographs of Denver's Broadway Park show how the sections of bleachers not under the infield grandstand left spectators without shade.

PIONEERS AND PLACES

Cobe Jones, pictured here in 1929, was a hometown hero in Denver. He played for two seasons for the Pittsburgh Pirates in addition to his semipro career in Colorado, which spanned some 15 years. In 1941, Jones managed the Western League's Denver Bears, and in his final game he appeared as a player and got a hit in his last professional at-bat.

The 1912 Western League pennant is being raised on opening day in 1913 at Broadway Park II. George Tebeau, wearing a bowler with a black topcoat and white tie, is seen facing the camera in the center of the photograph.

Also taken on opening day in 1913, this photograph shows ceremonial red, white, and blue bunting being hung from the clubhouse building. Note the onlookers perched high upon the field for a better vantage point.

In 1913, a crowd leaves Broadway Park II following the Denver Bears' opening day. Note the trolley cars ready to head back into downtown Denver.

Shown here are the 1901 St. Paul Saints, also known as "The Apostles." Players in this photograph include Jimmy Ryan (LF/MGR, third row, far left), Miller Huggins (2B, third row, second from back), Charlie Knepper (P), Parke Wilson (C, third row, third from left), Willie "Kid" McGill (P, sitting, holding baseball), Howard Holmes (C), Ed Holly (SS), Perry "Zaza" Werden (1B), Doc Parker (P/OF, second row, second from left), Jack Crooks (INF), Dave Brian (3B, in white cap), Pat Dillard (OF), and a player known only as Thomas (P). This photograph was taken at Broadway Park II on April 10, 1901. Huggins, also known as "Mighty Mite," or simply "Hug," went on to become a Hall of Fame player-manager for the St. Louis Cardinals and manager for the New York Yankees.

Shown here is a 1900 Denver Bears game at Broadway Park II. Note the antique vehicles in the outfield grass, an indication that this game was played in the dead-ball era. Even more than a century ago, billboard advertisements generated revenue.

Construction began on Merchants Park, located at 600 South Broadway Boulevard, in April 1922. It was razed in 1948. Baseball Hall of Famers who appeared at Merchants Park include Babe Ruth, James "Cool Papa" Bell, Rogers Hornsby, Buck Leonard, Johnny Mize, Satchel Paige, Lou Gehrig, Josh Gibson, Grover Cleveland Alexander, Oscar Charleston, and Bob Feller. Merchants Park hosted the Denver Post Tournament from 1922 until the park's closing in 1947. The photograph below was taken on December 21, 1928, looking north on Broadway Boulevard. The Montgomery Ward Building, the prominent structure in the background, stood for a number of decades after the park had been torn down.

This view from the main concourse at Merchants Park faces left field. The infield grandstand provided much-needed shade for paying attendees. By the mid-1920s, the park had become the home of the annual Denver Post Tournament and of the Denver Bears of the Western League. In 1930, this became the first ballpark in the Rocky Mountains region to install permanent lights. This led to much larger crowds attending games on weeknights and the beginning of nightly radio broadcasts and re-creations.

This photograph of Merchants Park was taken in February 1947. Note the dirt outfield, which was a nightmare for defenses to play on. Clearly visible is the original fence, which was made obsolete when the wall in left and center fields was moved in.

Broadway Park II is positioned with home plate at the corner of Sixth Avenue and Acoma Street. The right-field foul line ran fairly parallel to Sixth Avenue. Broadway Boulevard appears beyond the right-field fence, and Speer Boulevard and the Cherry Creek are located over the center-field wall. The field was reconfigured after the Cherry Creek was altered due to man-made construction and after expansion of the increasingly busy intersection of Sixth and Broadway.

Denver native Bert Niehoff (left) is pictured in 1929 before a spring-training game in Texas with National Baseball Hall of Fame manager John McGraw (center) and another Hall of Famer, catcher Ray Schalk. Known to have played to win in the 1919 World Series, Schalk was caught up in the subsequent Black Sox scandal. He possesses the lowest batting average of any Hall of Fame player but was inducted for his phenomenal defense behind the plate and his ability to handle pitchers.

In 1905, baseball fans watch the score being posted at the Denver Post Building. The contest this day was a road game between the Denver Bears and the Sioux City Sioux.

Broadway Park II, shown here on a windy day, was home to 10 of the first 11 Denver Post Tournaments. George Tebeau built the park in 1900 for the Denver Bears of the Western League. The facility was the equal of those in the big leagues at the time.

This 1909 photograph of Tom Hughes, who played for the New York Highlanders (later the New York Yankees), was taken at the Polo Grounds. Hughes, who hailed from Coal Creek, Colorado, pitched a no-hitter against the Pittsburgh Pirates in 1916. He is 25 years old here.

Jimmy Williams, seen here in 1903, played in Denver in 1896 while with the Pueblo Rovers of the Colorado State League. He went on to have a lengthy big-league career. Williams was born in St. Louis, but his family relocated to Colorado when he was young. The Williams family ran a tea and spice shop in Denver, and Jimmy learned baseball on the sandlots of the city before being signed by the Rovers.

The Colorado School of Mines team was managed by Burt Jones. Shown here are, from left to right, (first row) Davis, Rockwood, Strong, Turner, and Price; (second row) McGuire, Litchfield, Robinson, Thomas, Jones, Watson, Wilson, and Warren.

PIONEERS AND PLACES

The 1900 Denver Bears pose for a team photograph. Shown here are, from left to right, (first row) Harry "Klondike" Kane (P, OF); (second row) Charles Zeits (OF), James Vizard, Walter "Wizard" Preston (CF), Jack Sullivan (C), unidentified, and W.E. "Bill" Hickey (INF); (third row) Jack Holland (OF, INF), Joe Tinker (2B), Pop Eyler (P), Art "Buck" Weaver (UT), Tom "Tacks" Parrott (P/OF/1B), Pearl "Casey" Barnes (INF), and Eddie "Kid" Lewee (SS). The players are standing in front of the clubhouse in center field. Note that the date on the billboard, September 1880, refers not to the time of the photograph but to the contents of the advertisement.

Shown here in 1948 is Bears Stadium, which, between 1948 and 1994, was the home of the Class A and AAA Denver Bears as well as the Denver Zephyrs and Colorado Rockies. It was renamed Mile High Stadium in the 1960s and was expanded on three occasions. It became home to the NFL's Denver Broncos in 1960 and shortly thereafter was adorned with its famous bucking bronco, Bucky. The icon now resides atop the south stands of Sports Authority Field at Mile High Stadium.

This is a 1955 aerial photograph of Bears Stadium in Denver. Note the bed being prepared for the new "Valley Highway," also known as Interstate 25.

The new Denver Broncos stadium is under construction here around 2000 in the shadow of then current Mile High Stadium.

Byron Johnson (third from left), Buck O'Neil (fourth from left), and baseball historian Jay Sanford (second from right) sit with a number of Public Broadcasting Service employees while getting a tour of Coors Field in mid-construction.

Posing with a model of Coors Field in September 1994 are, from left to right, Roger Kinney (Colorado Rockies vice president), baseball ambassador Buck O'Neil (all-star player/manager for the Kansas City Monarchs), and Paula Colorosa (administration, Colorado Rockies).

Buck O'Neil (left) and Byron Johnson, teammates while playing for the Kansas City Monarchs, pose on the grass at Coors Field on September 5, 2000.

Keli McGregor, president of the Colorado Rockies, addresses the crowd in 2004 at the unveiling of the original home plate marker and corresponding sign commemorating the site of the original Bears stadium field.

At Merchants Park, Denver Bears owner Milt Ansfinger holds the leash on the team mascot (above) on opening day in April 1923. Ansfinger receives good-luck wreaths (below) as the Bears open the 1923 campaign against the Omaha Hogs.

2

THE DENVER POST
TOURNAMENT

The Denver Post Tournament was the city's crown jewel for sports and tourism. Beginning in 1915, teams made the trek to Denver in hopes of going home with the championship purse and accolades that came with the trophy. Above, the 1915 champions are, from left to right, Lloyd Winger (P), Charlie Jackson (P), ? O'Dell (1B), ? D'Armit (SS), ? Mattick (2B), Rolla "Lefty" Mapel (P), and R.D. Davis (business manager); below, are, from left to right, ? Bolton (3B), ? Gilmore (RF), Verne Garrett (LF), ? Harmon (SS), Dan Jones (CF), Lawrence Bolinger (C), and team captain Fred Finney (3B). Mapel went on to pitch in the big leagues in 1919 for the St. Louis Browns. He failed to record a single victory but did get one hit before being sent down.

This team from Olathe, Colorado, played in the Denver Post Tournament in 1925. The manager was Art Loper, and among the players was left fielder and pitcher Johny "Kid" West (first row, fourth from left). His son Robert West was a gifted Colorado baseball player who went on to play professionally in the early 1950s.

The Cheyenne Indians pose during the 1922 tournament. Shown are, from left to right, (first row) Junior Kellup (batboy); (second row) Jimmy Murray (SS), Reverend Schuetz (2B), Hal Newberry (OF), Al Cronland (2B), Elmer Brown (1B), Frank Provence (RF), Tom Blodgett (P), and Vincent Nick Carter (P); (third row) Eddie Murray (3B), Frank Petersen (CF), Big Ed McGlone (INF), Ed Gerrans (manager), Patton (C), Smirch (C), and John Pickett (P). This team, sponsored by the Havana Cigar Company, had 2,000 spectators traveling with them in attendance. The players were paid $88 each for the tournament. Cheyenne, Wyoming, was an exceptional baseball community dating back to the early 1870s. The Indians entered seven Denver Post Tournaments in the 1920s, winning the 1923 event.

UMPIRE NEWHOUSE, DICTATOR OF THE DIAMOND   BY GIBBONS

Frank Newhouse was an icon on the Denver sports scene for three decades. As an employee of the *Denver Post*'s circulation department, Newhouse and coworker Jabe Cassady developed the idea of the Denver Post Tournament in 1915. Newhouse officiated high school and collegiate basketball and baseball games. He was also a well-respected boxing referee on the Denver fight scene. In the first years of the tournament, Newhouse was the business manager and umpire for the event. He was also a "bird-dog" (volunteer) scout for a number of major-league teams over the years, signing many players to their first professional contracts.

Post Tourney Sketches---Done by Andrews

For over a decade, Doc Finch, or "Bird," entertained readers with his cartoons in the sports pages of the *Denver Post*. The characters in the cartoon at left represent the entrants in the 1916 Post Tournament as well as Colorado's pre–World War I economy. Farming, ranching, manufacturing, mining, tobacco production, and the military employed many Coloradans. The cartoon below is from 1919.

We Say It's Some Swell Dish

Area baseball fans were well rewarded during the 1920 Denver Post Tournament, when 14 former big-league players participated. Among the crowd favorites at Broadway Park II were three 20-game winners: Dave Davenport, Otto Hess, and Gene Packard. These cartoons are from 1921.

NOW FOR THE BIG NOISE　　　—By Doc Bird

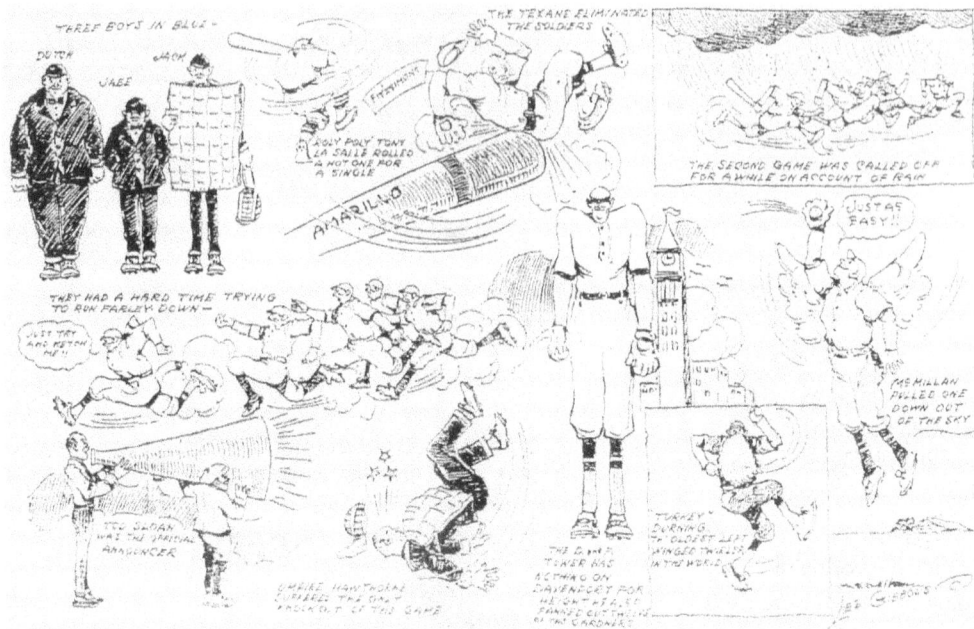

Shown here are Denver Post Tournament cartoons from 1923 and 1925. The Cheyenne Indians took first place in the 1923 tourney. In 1925, uniform numbers appeared on the backs of players' uniforms. A first in baseball, this was done to help tournament enthusiasts follow individual players more closely. Unlike number assignments today, at that time every player in the tournament was assigned a unique number, so that no two players, even on different teams, shared the same number. As a result, some players' numbers ran to three digits, as there were over 100 participants in 1925.

Babe Ruth (left) and Otto Floto meet atop "the house the Ruth built," Yankee Stadium, in 1925. Floto, the *Denver Post* sports editor, rose to prominence as a highly regarded member of the media due to his incredible acumen regarding baseball and prizefighting. He helped found and establish the Denver Post Tournament.

This cartoon depicts the gravestone of George Tebeau. Many of this great baseball man's contributions have been forgotten. He was instrumental in founding today's American League and possessed an exceptional eye for talented ballplayers. He built Broadway Park II and played on Denver's first organized ball club, the Denvers, in 1886.

Busload of Talent for Post's Tournament

A BUSLOAD of baseball talent rolled into Denver Wednesday. The bus, from Wichita, Kan., contained members of the Wichita Advertisers baseball team, who came to Denver to take part in The Denver Post annual baseball tournament, which opened at Broadway park Thursday. The picture shows them just after they reached Denver, rarin' to go. Their first tournament game will be played Saturday, when they meet the fast Lubbock, Tex., nine.

This *Wichita Advertiser* article highlights a team that traveled to Denver from Wichita, where the National Baseball Congress Tournament is held annually. In 1966, 1967, 1975, and 1978, the Boulder Collegians were national champions of this famous competition. Bus Campbell, legendary pitching coach and scout in Colorado, and his team was once invited to play in the famous Midnight Sun Game, held annually on the summer solstice in Fairbanks, Alaska, against the Alaska Goldpanners. They escaped Alaska with a 5-2 victory and headed back to Colorado on June 22, 1969.

This program cover is for the 1925 Denver Post Tournament. The featured teams that year were from the following cities: Lubbock, Texas; Parco, Wyoming; Amarillo, Texas; Olathe, Kansas; Cheyenne, Wyoming; Grant, Nebraska; Clear Vision Pump, Kansas; and Fort Russell, Wyoming. Also participating were local teams: the Denver Elitchs, the Gardner Motors Ball Club, and the Fitzsimmons Ball Club.

The 1934 Kansas City Monarchs pose for a team portrait. Shown here are, from left to right, (seated) unidentified batboy; (first row) Frank Duncan, "Bullet Joe" Rogan, Dink Mothel, Sam Bankhead, Newt Allen, Newt Joseph, and Eddie Dwight; (second row) Willie Foster, George Giles, Tom Young, Turkey Stearns, Chet Brewer, Sam Crawford, John Donaldson, Charley Beverly, and Andy Cooper. The first Negro League team to appear in the Denver Post Tournament, this Monarchs squad fell just short of winning the championship, edged out by Satchel Paige and Grover Cleveland Alexander's House of David team.

Unidentified House of David players flank House of David Manager Grover Cleveland "Pete" Alexander, one of baseball's all-time greats. Alexander led three teams to the Denver Post Tournament, winning one championship in 1934 by defeating the Kansas City Monarchs. (Courtesy of the Rucker Archive.)

A 1936 Negro League all-star contingent won the 1936 Denver Post Tournament. This may very well be the greatest baseball team to ever set foot in Denver, including the 2007 World Series champion Boston Red Sox, who clinched the title at Coors Field. This all-star team was comprised of the best Homestead Grays, Pittsburgh Crawfords, and Baltimore Elite Giants. That same year, future Hall of Famer Rogers Hornsby played for the Bay Refiners and Grover Cleveland Alexander, also destined for Cooperstown, managed the House of David team. Shown here are, from left to right, (first row) Paul Hardy, Bob Griffith, Satchel Paige, Ray Brown, Sam Streeter, Josh Gibson, and ? Horne (batboy); (second row) ? Whitton (trainer), Buck Leonard, Chet Williams, "Cool Papa" Bell, Felton Snow, Boisy Marshall (manager), and Jim Taylor; (third row) H.S. Posey (business manager), Sammy Hughes, Vic Harris, Bill Wright, and ? Hart.

One of the greatest American athletes to ever grace a field, Hall of Fame inductee "Bullet Joe" Rogan was highly regarded for his ability to both play the outfield and pitch, much like Babe Ruth and Smokey Joe Wood. One statistical compilation shows Rogan winning more games than any other pitcher in Negro League history and ranking fourth in career batting average. Casey Stengel called Rogan one of the greatest, if not the greatest, pitcher who ever lived.

In 1934, future National Baseball Hall of Fame inductee Norman "Turkey" Stearns appeared with the Kansas City Monarchs. He is pictured here in 1936 while playing for the Chicago American Giants. In the 1938 East versus West Negro League All-Star Game, Stearns's friend Byron Johnson broke his only bat. Knowing this, Stearns loaned a spare bat to Johnson with a clause stating that if he were to get a hit, he could keep the bat. With such ingenuity, Stearns motivated his teammates and put himself a distant second to what always came first: the team.

Eddie Dwight was an exceptionally fast outfielder. His speed and base-running ability was often compared to that of Cool Papa Bell, who was widely regarded as one of the fastest men to ever step foot on a baseball diamond. Dwight was a contact hitter with zero to little power, but he was an excellent bunter with great hit-and-run ability. This made him an ideal table setter, and he regularly hit second for the majority of the 1930s for the Kansas City Monarchs. Dwight spent his entire 13-year career with Midwestern teams. In 1962, his son Eddie Dwight Jr. became the first African American candidate selected by NASA for astronaut training. His son also gained notoriety for being the sculptor of "Hammer'" Hank Aaron's statue at Turner Field in Atlanta.

The 1937 Trujillo All-Stars were a Negro League all-star team. At the time of this photograph, the players had just won the Caribbean championship. In 1937, the team also won the equally prestigious Denver Post Tournament.

The 1937 Trujillo All-Stars pose for a team photograph. Shown here are, from left to right, (first row) Enrique Lantiqua, Leroy Matlock, Julio Vasquez, James "Cool Papa" Bell, Sam Bankhead, Silvio Garcia, and Cho-Cho Correa; (second row) Lazaro Salazar, Don Jose Enrique Ayubar, and Satchel Paige; (third row) Josh Gibson, Chester Williams, Antonio Caselnos, Rodolpho Fernandez, Robert Griffith, Perucho Cepeda, and William Perkins. The team was sponsored by the president of the Dominican Republic, Rafeal Trujillo, who took the game very seriously. According to Satchel Paige, the Americans were watched closely: "If we went swimming we were chaperoned by soldiers. We had soldiers on our hotel floors too and Trujillo gave orders that anyone in town selling us whiskey would be shot." Peruch Cepeda, nicknamed "The Bull," is the father of National Baseball Hall of Fame inductee Orlando Cepeda (also known as "The Baby Bull").

The Ethiopian Clowns Will Be Here Thursday Night!

The Ethiopian Clowns were an entrant in the 1939, 1940, and 1941 Denver Post Tournaments. Often referred to as "the Harlem Globetrotters of Baseball," this team was founded in Florida in the mid-1930s and eventually made its home in Indianapolis, Indiana. It was a 12-year member of Negro League baseball before becoming essentially defunct following the 1954 season. "Hammerin' " Hank Aaron signed his first professional contract with the Clowns before it was purchased by Roland Hemond's then employer, the Boston Braves. Team members would often wear grass "hula" skirts in an effort to stay cooler than their opponents.

Otto Flotto (left) and Jack Dempsey pose for this "teacher-student" photograph at the *Denver Post*'s offices in 1928. Flotto, instrumental in establishing the Denver Post Tournament, was so highly regarded on a national level that he was widely seen as the "grandfather" of American sports journalism.

Nick Urban displays the winner's check and the first-place trophy for being the 1939 Denver Post Tournament champion.

Shown here at the 1946 Denver Post Tournament check presentation are, from left to right Hughie Morris, manager of the second-place Rogers Jewelry team; Jim Garramone, manager of the first-place M&O Cigars team; Joe Cianilio, of Joe Albert Clothiers; and Jack Carberry, the *Denver Post* sports editor.

This photograph was taken at the Eighth Avenue Gym in Greeley, Colorado, on February 7, 1932, on the occasion of a match between Harry Bostron and ? Davis. Shown are, from left to right, (first row) Connie Wills, Solidger Scotty, Don Bostron, and Mr. Kitts, the *Greeley Tribune* sportswriter; (second row) Joe Jacobs (Max Schmeling's manager), Earl Blick, Harry Bostron, former heavyweight champion Jack Dempsey, Ray Morris (Diaz's manager), unidentified, and Poss Parsons, the *Denver Post* sports editor largely responsible for integrating the Denver Post Tournament decades before Branch Rickey integrated Major League Baseball.

The House of David team featured two future Hall of Famers: Satchel Paige and his manager, Grover Cleveland Alexander. The House of David religious colony did not allow African Americans as members, but that did not prevent its baseball team from signing the Pittsburgh Crawfords' famed battery of Cy Perkins and Paige. The team won the 1934 tournament.

Alexander to Lead With His Ace!

GROVER CLEVELAND ALEXANDER.

Grover Cleveland Alexander, one of the greatest major league pitchers of all time and now manager of House of David, will send Satchel Paige, outstanding Negro pitcher in baseball, to the mound against Eason Oilers of Enid, Okla., in Monday night's game in THE POST tournament. Alkbo playing with the Bearded Beauties, neither sports any facial foliage. Alex contract stipulates he doesn't have to wear a beard while Paig just joined the team for the tournament.

ORRL PAIGE.

Leroy "Satchel" Paige is seen here in 1940 while playing in the Cuban Winter League. Paige loved coming to Denver so much that in the early 1980s Jim Burress would have Paige pitch to Denver media at Mile High Stadium dressed in a full Denver Bears uniform just so that those lucky folks could say they got a hit off of the right-handed Hall of Famer.

The great Satchel Paige is pictured here in June 1952 while playing for the St. Louis Browns. Owner Bill Veeck thought it clever to provide a leather recliner for the aging Paige. Les Moss (center) and Bob Cain are seated next to the "Satch" chair.

Heroes of Victories by Duncan and Pampa Sluggers!

LESLIE MUNNS

DUTCH PRATHER

SAMMY BAUGH

JOE HASSLER

GEHRIG BOOSTS WRONG

Munns' pitching and Hassler's hitting led the Halliburton Cementers to victory over Minnesota Mines. Prather and Baugh were the big guns of Pampa's trouncing of Kansas City, in POST tournament games Saturday at Merchants park.

TWO GREAT

The 1937 Denver Post Tournament was won by the Ciudad Trujillo/Negro League All-Star Team. "Slingin' " Sammy Baugh, the future Washington Redskins football great, played in the 1937 event, as did a handful of future baseball Hall of Famers.

Power hitter Judy Cline played in the 1932 Denver Post Tournament. Cline was one of only three players to hit a ball over the center-field wall at Merchants Park; the other two were Babe Ruth and Josh Gibson.

3

SEMIPRO, COLLEGIATE, AMATEUR, AND YOUTH

The Denver High School baseball team is seen here around 1888. The team wore blue uniforms and had its very own umpire, shown here seated in the center. A student named Harsh was listed as the pitcher, and Hannington was listed as catcher.

The Denver High School team poses for a photograph around 1890. The school was located just north of East Colfax in what today would be called Uptown, between Capitol Hill and Five Points.

The August 2, 1891, *Rocky Mountain News* reported, "There will be two games today. . . . There was no game between the Sanden and Pueblo's at Broadway Park yesterday as the rain which fell just after noon completely soaked the grounds and it was decided to postpone the game until this morning when the game intended for yesterday will be played off. Another game will be played as advertised at 3:30 in the afternoon both teams have first class batteries and the games will be good ones. Ladies will be admitted free to both games, The Sanden souvenir photographs will be presented to each lady attending. Sandens by position Caplen—Pitcher, Cotton—Catcher, Little—Firstbase, McAulifle—secondbase, Preston–Third, Allen–Short, Pink–Leftfield, McLaughlin–Center field, Walker–Right field."

The 1892 Colorado School of Mines baseball team poses for a photograph. Shown are, from left to right, (sitting) George Kennedy, George Schneider, Charles McMahan, Lester Hartzell, unidentified, Frank Aller, and Wallace Stephens; (standing) ? Bohn, George (or Joe) Kimball (manager), Edmund Rowe.

The Sanden Electric Base Ball Club is seen here around 1895 in Denver, Colorado. According to the *National Police Gazette* of New York City, the Sanden Electrics club was one of the top amateur baseball teams in the United States. Bert Davis owned a "smoke shop" in downtown Denver and played and managed several successful baseball teams, including the Gulfs in Denver. Left fielder Willoughby was one of several players from the well-known Willoughby family that played baseball in Denver between 1862 and the early 1900s.

The Gulfs Railroad team is seen here in 1896. Posing for the team photograph are McCausland, Hudson, Gerhardt, Lawrence, Hastings, Shaber, Stoney, Cotton, Schuable, Burke, Zeitz, and Nagle.

This 1897 photograph shows the Colorado School of Mines baseball team. The players include Fred C. Steinhauer, Mullins, Steele, Lempke, Price, Burdick, Proutt, Ball, Truett, Burkett, Stoney, and E.J. Moody (manager). Lempke chose an engineering career over professional baseball.

Members of the 1898 Denver University Law School baseball club gather for a team portrait. Shown here are, from left to right, (first row) William Sprangler (SS), George Post (2B), Floyd Lilyard (3B, captain), Dudley Strikland (C), and two unidentified men; (second row) George Humphrey (P and manager), Commodore Jackson (RF), Newton Gandy (LF), unidentified, Walter Schuyler (CF), and two unidentified men. Among the men whose identities cannot be matched with persons in the photograph are Gilbert Mann (1B), James Anglum, and Watt Sheldon.

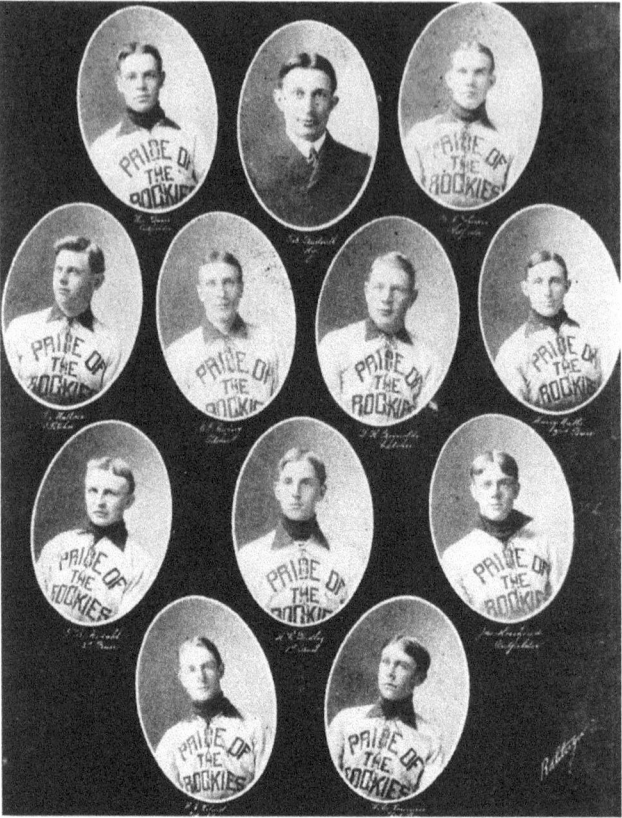

This Colorado all-star team, the Pride of the Rockies, featured players of high caliber prior to their reaching the semiprofessional ranks.

The Fire Clay Company, like many successful small businesses in the area, sponsored competitive teams in Denver around the turn of the century. Such sponsorship was an effective means of advertising and associated the business with the local community.

Seen here in Denver in 1901 is the Spalding House Sporting Goods Company junior team. Befitting a club sponsored by a sporting-goods company, these young players are deftly equipped. Note the early chest protector in the lower center of the photograph. Presumably a young men's all-star team, it was sponsored by the nation's key baseball-equipment manufacturing company.

The 1902 Old Homestead team was the Colorado, Utah, and New Mexico champion, winning 37 out of 38 games—30 of them away from Denver. Shown are, from left to right, (top row) W. Good and E. Ewing (second row) M. Mesch, J. Good (manager), W.J. Mickelham (financial backer), and J. Galgano; (third row) T. Birkedahl, W. McGilvray, and C. Roberts; (bottom row) Bert Neihoff and N. Burgess. Neihoff had a long stay on the Colorado baseball scene as a big leaguer for five years with the Phillies, Reds, Cardinals, and Giants. The Louisville, Colorado, native made Denver his off-season home and lived there for much of his post-retirement life.

The Overland Cotton Mill baseball team is shown here around 1903. The mill was located on East Evans Avenue. Among the players shown here is Charles Melvin Reed, the father of talented Denver baseball player Mel Reed, who went on to play professionally.

The Denver Tramway Nine club is seen here around 1910. The term "tramway" was generally not used in the United States, but one began operating in Denver and was incorporated in 1886, at which time it quickly began finding ways to also incorporate itself with baseball.

Local 121 and 68 of the International Brotherhood of Electrical Workers in Denver, Colorado, sported a baseball team. Shown here are Charles Oliver (manager, in mustache), W. Miller (2B, captain), Frank Burrigan (C), Marion Steck (P), Ira Steck (1B), Nelson (infield), Claude Williamson (RF), Tommy McLean (CF), Teddy Lake (LF), Jaime Bowden (SS), and Johnnie Celland (3B).

The Fort Logan baseball team poses during the 1913 season. Shown here are, from left to right, (first row) Fred "Cap" Waller (C, captain), Bill "Soup" Allen (2B), Charles "Lucky" Baker (P), unidentified, August "Gussie" Uhl (SS); (second row) Johnny Newman (LF), Delancy "Tod" Sloan (P), Matthew "Matty" Salinger (C), Col. George Van Deusen, Lt. E.M. Norton (manager), Clifford Shaf (1B), Fred "Pep" Wells (3B), and William "Spud" Murphy (RF).

The Fort Logan baseball team is seen around 1913 with its mascot poodle, which is standing at attention with the soldier-ballplayers. This team was comprised of the best talent serving on the base. Today, the site is home to the South Lakewood Army Base.

Children sit beside the Archer Canal in west Denver, seemingly before or after a ball game, in 1914.

The A.B. HIRSCHFELD BASEBALL TEAM 1915

The Hirschfeld Press team assembles in 1915. Crouching in front are A.B. Hirschfeld and batboy Eddie Hirschfeld. The players are, from left to right, Fishman, Caminoli, Serafini, Poland, G. Spector, Healy, Pringle, Grant, and Oppenhiem.

The A. B. HIRSCHFELD BASEBALL TEAM 1916

The Hirschfeld Press Young Men's baseball team is seen here in 1916. The photograph was taken at Broadway Park II.

The University
of Colorado is
preparing to play
the Fort Logan
team at Denver's
Broadway Park
II around 1918.

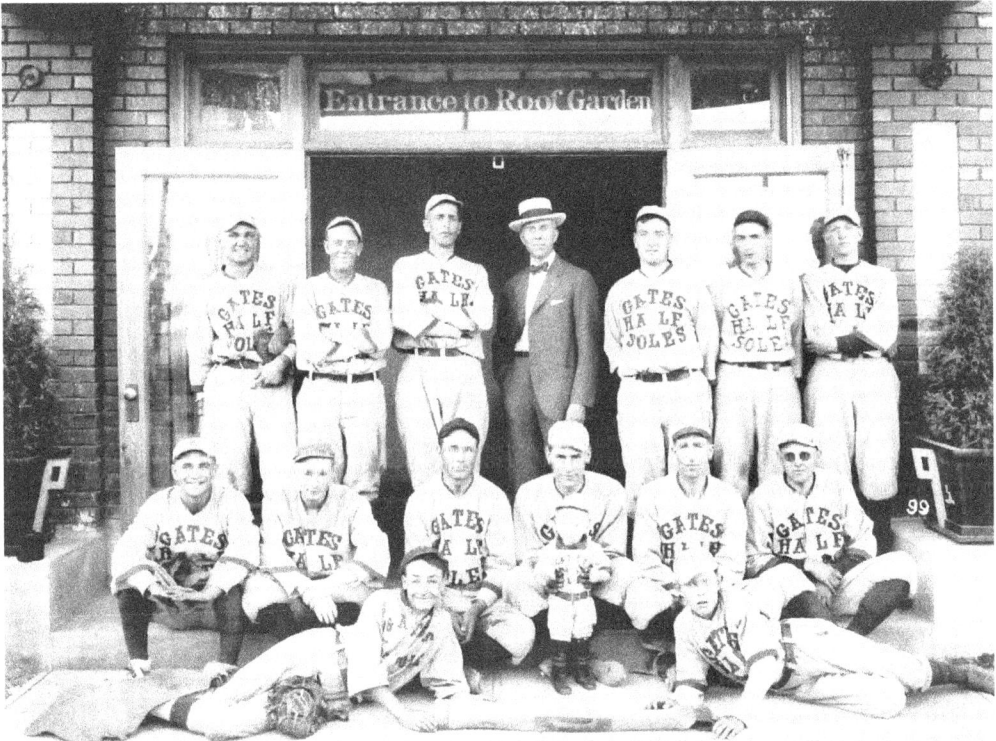

The Gates Half Soles baseball team poses with Charles Cassius Gates (back row, center). He and the Gates family were very successful in the rubber business. The Gates Rubber Company became one of the nation's leaders in petroleum-based products. Coincidentally, the Gates Rubber Factory came to stand for many decades very near the site of Merchants Park.

Park Kenney appeared in the Denver Post Tournament as a player-manager with the Boulder Collegians. This smooth-fielding infielder hit over .300 in four Post classics. His son Roger was a middle infielder for the University of Colorado. No individual was more instrumental than Roger in helping Colorado and the Rockies franchise in getting voter approval to build Coors Field.

PARK KENNEY
Captain

The Broomfield Lumber Company baseball club is seen here in 1927. The amateur men's team competed in the Denver League and played non-sanctioned ball games against beet-farm teams from northern Colorado.

ラスアニマス 旭 丹 球 團 AUG 12-/928.

A team of Japanese American youth poses for a photograph north of downtown Denver on August 12, 1928.

Shown here is the Fort Logan 2nd Engineers baseball team. Military units such as this went on to be part of the Army Corps of Engineers. The photograph was taken in Lakewood in the early spring of 1928.

PIGGLY WIGGLY BEATS BOULDER COLLEGIANS, 11-7

The *Denver Post* headline on August 12, 1929, indicates that baseball has always been a top story in the Mile High City. Whether national or local, baseball has been front and center on the sports scene for much of Denver's existence.

The Kunitomos, a semiprofessional baseball team, is pictured here in 1920 in an orchard believed to be just west of East High School. Dr. Kunitomo was a surgeon who owned and operated the team for a number of years.

Denver's Goalstone Brothers Jewelers team poses for a photograph. Tom Albright is standing on the far left, and Lefty Banks is kneeling on the far right.

The 1930 White Elephants were Denver's first black semiprofessional team. Shown posing in the above photograph are, from left to right, (first row) Ike Bell, Willard Stevenson, unidentified batboy, Joe Tucker, and Theodore Johnson; (second row) A.H.W. Ross, Red Threats, "Boogie Woogie" Pardue, Logan Harper, "Little Johnny" (scorekeeper), and George Walker; (third row) Bill Carey, Lefty Banks, Robert Clay, Tom "Pistol Pete" Albright, Ed Steward, Reginald Cooper, and Fleming Von Dickershon. Albright played professionally for the New York Baccarat Giants (1929) and the New York Cubans (1934) of the Negro League. During a Denver Post Tournament game on August 2, 1934, he struck out 15 Kansas City Monarchs in a pitching duel with the great Chet Brewer.

The Baily Underhill Company sponsored boys' and girls' baseball teams in Denver for many years, providing recreation and competition for area kids of the Mile High City.

This 1938 photograph, taken at Elitch Gardens, shows, from left to right, Coors players Bud Cabble (P), George Anderson (SS), Roy Byers (P), Marion Payne (RF), and Ben Pister (C). Due to a lack of clubhouse facilities, a player is changing his uniform in the relative privacy of some trees.

The Rogers Square Deal Jewelers team poses in 1939. Over the years, this company sponsored many different clubs in various leagues and were always involved in community baseball in different capacities.

Art Unger, seen here in 1939, played for Denver's K&B Packers. He was a favorite with the fans at Merchants Park. A long ball–hitting outfielder, Unger played primarily for the K&B Packers and for the Coors Brewers. A diverse athlete, he also starred in basketball for the University of Colorado Buffaloes. "Big Art" wore his spectacles at the plate as well as in the field.

Eddie Vogel, a catcher for the Coors Brewers, slides back into first base. Meyer Shapiro is the first baseman for the K&B Packers in a game at Merchants Park in 1939. Close-up action shots like this one were possible at a time when press photographers were granted much more freedom of movement. Today, with the advent of the telephoto lens, photographers are relegated to more distant vantage points.

Former big leaguer Cobe Jones (left) looks to be flashing signs in this photograph taken at Golden Field in 1940.

In this 1940 photograph, George Anderson (left) and Jim Garramone (center) accept the Pueblo Colorado Tournament championship trophy at Runyon Field. The Coors team was highly competitive, rarely losing when traveling the state of Colorado.

The Home Owned Stores team featured a handful of future Negro League players. It competed in the Denver League against the White Elephants. The site of this 1933 photograph is believed to be City Park.

HOME OWNED STORES BASEBALL TEAM - 1933

Art Unger was a superb semiprofessional baseball player in the 1940s. He played for the Coors Brewers and the K&B Packers at Merchants Park.

Kids in Denver turned out by the hundreds on the first day of practice for the Old Timers League in June 1941. Here, Charlie McGlone is giving instruction to the young men in attendance.

Jim Garramone, pictured here next to the team bus, managed the Coors Brewery traveling semiprofessional team in the 1940s.

The Coors Brewery team, Colorado's semiprofessional champions, poses for a photograph in Pueblo after the championship game at Runyon Field. Shown here are, from left to right, (first row) Jim Garramone (manager), Lou Pastore (batboy), ? Schmidt, Leonard Hawkins, Art Unger, Bruno Konopka, and Harry Hallman; (second row) Johnny Smith, Roy Byers, Cecil Scheffel, Bob Eaton, George Anderson, Gene Ater, Al Kavanaugh, George Hall, Dick Hotton, and Sticks Stonich.

Dick Hotton slides safely into home plate after rounding the bases on an inside-the-park home run at Merchants Park in 1940.

The outfielders of the M&O Cigars team are Ernie Roth (left), John Lloyd (center), and Al Zarilla. This photograph was taken at Merchants Park in 1942. Zarilla had a 10-year major-league career playing for the St. Louis Browns, the Boston Red Sox, and the Chicago White Sox. He had an incredible 1950 campaign, compiling a .915 OPS (on-base plus slugging percentages) while playing right field. Ted Williams was his teammate in left field.

M&O Cigar pitchers, seen here in 1942, are Bob Peterson (left), Jim Conboy (center), and Porter Vaughn, who played for the Philadelphia Athletics in 1940 and 1941 before going off to war. Vaughn's manager, Connie Mack, allowed him to return in 1946, but Vaughn was not successful after his years away from the professional ranks.

The 1942 M&O Cigar infield was composed of, from left to right, Roy Byers, George Anderson, Gene Atter, and Dick Hotton.

John Kestel (left) and Bennie Pister, seen here around 1945, were catchers on the M&O Cigar team.

The M&O Cigar club won the first post–World War II Denver Post Tournament, in 1946. Jim Garramone's team featured former major leaguers Lee Grissom and Roy "Beau" Bell. Shown from left to right are (seated) Junior Garramone (batboy); (first row) Jim Garramone, George Anderson, Ray Cairns, Al Kavanaugh, Jim Queen, Gene Ater, Jim Conboy, Bob "Lefty" Cairns, and Lou Hansen; (second row) Grissom, Art Unger, Bob Justman, Dick Hotton, unidentified, Bob Peterson, Bell, Darrell Geisert, and Jim Otto.

This photograph reveals the lighting structures that had been in place since 1930 at Merchants Park. Lights were featured there long before Crosley Field made them available in the National League. The smokestack behind the home plate grandstand still stands today, on South Broadway just north of Interstate 25.

A play at the plate is captured at Elitch Gardens Ballpark around 1949. Elitch Gardens Amusement Park provided entertainment in many different forms, from ball games to carousels to roller coasters.

4

DENVER BEARS

Bears Stadium, seen here in 1948, was the home of the Class A and Triple-A Denver Bears teams, as well as the Denver Zephyrs, from 1948 to 1992. It was renamed Mile High Stadium in the 1960s and was expanded on three occasions. This was to become the home of the Denver Broncos in 1960.

Seen here on June 9, 1960, at Bears Stadium are *Denver Post* sportswriter Frank Haraway (left), Bears coach Vern Rapp (rear center), Post sports editor Chuck Garrity (front center), and Bears manager Charlie Metro.

Tom Grieve (left), Del Wilber (center), and Richie Scheinblum were part of the Denver Bears team in 1971.

Denver Bears Marv Thornberry (left) and Ralph Houk (right) pose with *Denver Post* sports editor Frank Harraway in the spring of 1955.

Craig Nettles, a Denver Bear in 1968, became a world champion with the New York Yankees in 1977 and 1978. One of his Yankee teammates was Colorado product Rich "Goose" Gossage.

The top brass of the Denver Bears and the Chicago White Sox gather as the two teams formed an affiliation in 1975. Shown here are, from left to right, (seated) White Sox general manager Roland Hemond, Bears manager Loren Babe, and White Sox manager Chuck Tanner; (standing) Bears general manager Jim Burris and White Sox farm director C.V. Davis.

Denver Bears manager Mike Gazella argues with umpire Russ Kimpel in a 1948 game against Des Moines. In the background are, from left to right, George Genovese, Al Yaylian, and Buddy Phillips. Gazella was a Yankee teammate of Babe Ruth.

Bob Howsam, seen here in 1950, owned the Denver Bears long before he served as general manager of the 1975 and 1976 world champion "Big Red Machine" Cincinnati Reds. A movement is under way to elect Howsam into the executives wing of the National Baseball Hall of Fame, and deservedly so. Were it not for Howsam's push to bring major-league baseball to Denver in the late 1950s, the famous "South Stands" of Mile High Stadium would never have been built. The Phipps Construction Company built the stands initially, it seemed, in vain. But the seating section ultimately became infamous when the Denver Broncos and its "Orange Crush" defense were in their 1970s glory.

Whitey Herzog, the Hall of Fame manager of the Kansas City Royals and St. Louis Cardinals, had a spectacular 1955 season while playing for the Bears. Herzog, 23 at the time, hit 24 doubles and 21 home runs for the New York Yankees' highest affiliate.

National Baseball Hall of Fame manager Tommy Lasorda, seen here in 1955 with the Brooklyn Dodgers, pitched for the Denver Bears in 1956 and part of the 1957 season.

Bobby Richardson played second base for the Denver Bears in 1956 and then for the New York Yankees for 10 years, winning three World Series and even a World Series MVP (1960), albeit for the losing team—the only time it has ever happened.

A
AA
American
Association

WESTERN
LEAGUE
Champions
1954

This photograph of the 1954 Denver Bears, promoting the 1955 season, features Earl Weaver (first row, fourth from left). The second baseman went on to become the manager of the Baltimore Orioles, winning the World Series in 1970. He was elected to the National Hall of Fame in 1996. First baseman Butch McCord (first row, second from right) was a star in the Negro Leagues prior to playing for the Denver Bears.

Colorado first lady Ann Love threw out the first pitch in a game between the Washington Senators and the Denver Bears on June 9, 1970. Seen here with Love are Bears manager Whitey Kurowski (left) and Ted Williams. The first lady threw out the opening-day ceremonial first pitch for several seasons.

This is a 1955 Denver Bears holiday card. Boulder-area resident Herb Plews is in the third row, fourth from the left. Also among those pictured are the manager, Ralph Houk (third row, far right), coach Johnny Pesky (first row, center), Whitey Herzog (second row, third from left), and Marv Thornberry (second row, second from right).

Bears Stadium was erected in 1948. It served as the home to the Denver Bears and Zephyrs (A/Triple-A), 1948–1992; Denver Broncos (AFL/NFL), 1960–2000; Denver Gold (USFL), 1983–1985; Colorado Rockies (MLB), 1993–1994; Colorado Rapids (MLS), 1996–2001; Colorado Caribous (NASL), 1978; and Denver Dynamos (NASL), 1974–1975.

Red Ruffing (right) is pictured here with Bob Feller. Ruffing was the Denver Bears pitching coach. When he retired as a player, he had more wins than any pitcher in the history of Yankee Stadium. He was eventually passed by Whitey Ford. In May 2008, the Rocky Mountain chapter of the Society for American Baseball Research held a 50-year reunion of the New York Yankees and the Denver Bears at the Denver Athletic Club. In attendance were Ryne Duren, Norm Siebern, Boulder-area resident Herb Plews, World Series perfectionist Don Larson, Johnny Blanchard, and Ralph Terry.

Continental League officials gather in Minneapolis in 1959 to publicize a new "major league." Shown here are, from left to right, William Shea, the New York organizer; Wheelock Whitney, representing Minneapolis; J.W. Bateson, Dallas; Dwight Davis, New York; Craig Cullinan, Houston; Bob Howsam, Denver; Amon Carter Jr., Fort Worth–Dallas; Danny Mendez, Toronto; and Branch Rickey, the energetic 79-year-old league president. Buffalo later became the final member to complete the league. It is believed that were it not for this group spearheading competition to the American and National Leagues, expansion would not have happened as quickly as it did, beginning in the early 1960s.

Members of the 1957 Denver Bears Triple-A/ Little World Series championship team are, from left to right, "Marvelous Marv" Thornberry, the flame-throwing Ryne Duren, and Norm Siebern.

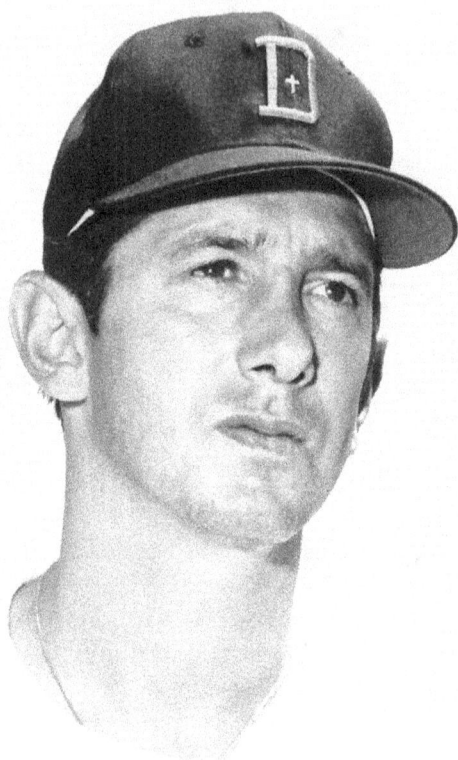

Billy Martin managed the 1968 Denver Bears, then a Minnesota farm club, to a 73-72 record. One year later, he managed the Minnesota Twins to a phenomenal 97-65 first-place finish, only to fall short to the Earl Weaver–led Baltimore Orioles for the 1969 American League championship. This was "the only job I wasn't fired from," said Billy Martin, referring to his managerial stint with the Denver Bears. While in Denver, Martin played under longtime baseball man Jim Burris, who was at the time the general manager of both the Denver Bears and the Denver Broncos.

Felipe Alou managed the Denver Bears in 1981. After his playing days, Alou began his outstanding managerial career with the Bears, a Montreal affiliate. Bob Burris mentioned that his father, Jim, had paid Alou the grandest of compliments, saying, "Felipe Alou is incapable of telling a lie."

Shown here in 1973 are Otis Thornton (left), Jim Williams (center), and James Rodney Richard. In four games started for the Denver Bears in 1974, J.R. Richard threw three complete game shutouts and allowed zero earned runs in 33 total innings. His fastball had been clocked at 100 miles an hour before being called up to Houston.

Jerry Manuel, a member of the 1980 Denver Bears, won the Manager of the Year Award in 2000 with the Chicago White Sox. Manuel managed for nine years in the big leagues, with Chicago in the American League and New York Mets in the National League.

Tim "Rock" Raines, along with Andre Dawson and Gary Carter, went on to have a legendary career for the Montreal Expos after playing in Denver. He played for the Bears in 1980.

Brad Mills, seen here in 1981, was a third baseman for the Denver Bears. In 2011, he became manager of the Houston Astros, joining former teammates Jerry Manuel and Terry Francona as major-league managers.

Terry Francona, currently the Cleveland Indians skipper, became immortal in Boston for leading the Red Sox to two world championships in 2004 and 2007. The latter World Series was clinched in Denver. Francona, a first-round draft pick in 1980, spent very little time in the minor leagues. Pictured here in 1981 during his rookie year in Montreal, Terry played in 93 games that season for the Denver Bears.

Bryn Smith was the starting pitcher for the Colorado Rockies in its inaugural season opener at Mile High Stadium. He had a 13-year career in the big leagues; his final season coincided with the Rockies' first year in existence.

Bob Gebhardt is seen here in a Denver Bears uniform in 1981. Gebhardt, the minor-league pitching instructor for the Montreal Expos, became the first general manager of the Colorado Rockies. Bob continues to call Denver home, though he has been working in the front office of the Arizona Diamondbacks for many years.

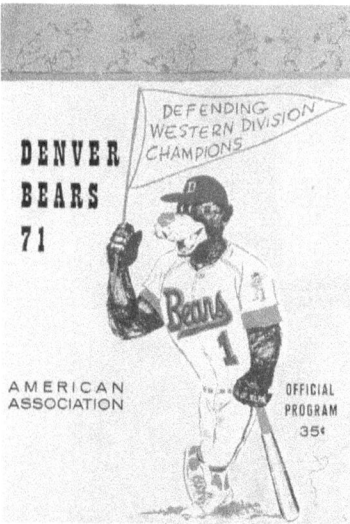

The 1971 Washington Senators–affiliated Denver Bears ball club was sprinkled with future major-league ballplayers, such as Jeff Burroughs, Tom Grieve, and a 28-year-old Richie Scheinblum. Scheinblum had 145 hits in 106 games, 25 home runs, 31 doubles, 10 triples, a .388 average, and an on-base percentage of .490, which is an outstanding season in any league. (Courtesy of the Rucker Archive.)

Bears Stadium sold out when it hosted the 1956 American Association All-Star Game. The success of the Denver Bears spawned Denver's football team. The Denver Broncos were founded in August 1959, when minor-league baseball owner Bob Howsam was awarded the American Football League's charter franchise in Denver. Howsam had originally sought to expand the NFL in Denver but was snubbed by George Halas, the National Football League's owner leader at the time. That slight led Howsam and four others to begin a rival league, the American Football League, which began play the following year in 1960.

5

BARNSTORMERS AND MORE LOCAL LEGENDS

In late October 1922, Babe Ruth (left) and Bob Meusel of the New York Yankees came through Denver and Pueblo. As Ruth's home runs increased, so did his celebrity. An attraction wherever he went, Ruth never shied away from the camera or notoriety.

Babe Ruth (left) and Lou Gehrig pose during a barnstorming tour in 1927. Their uniforms read, "Bustin' Babes" and "Larrupin Lou's."

Onlookers gawk as Babe Ruth takes batting practice at Merchants Park in 1927. Lou Gehrig is signing autographs in the background.

Josh Gibson, often referred to as the "Black Babe Ruth," was one of the greatest catchers and power hitters of all time. Gibson, who passed away at the early age of 35, was credited with hitting over 800 home runs. Some observers even went so far as to call Babe Ruth the "White Josh Gibson." He hit a storied home run at Merchants Park that went over the center-field wall, nearly 500 feet in distance.

"Cool Papa" Bell, shown here early in his career while playing for the St. Louis Stars, often came through Denver while on barnstorming trips. He famously played in the Denver Post Tournament in 1936.

BARNSTORMERS AND MORE LOCAL LEGENDS

Dizzy Dean (second from left), who played in Denver during Victory League play, is pictured here while playing for the Tulsa Drillers in 1941.

"The Ghost," Oliver Hazzard Marcelle, was one of the greatest third basemen to ever play the game. His defensive skills were second to none, and he could fairly be compared to Brooks Robinson. An exceptional hitter, Marcelle, along with Poss Parsons, is credited with integrating the Denver Post Tournament in 1934.

OLIVER "THE GHOST" MARCELLE

1897 — 1949

"BASEBALL'S BEST PROFESSIONAL THIRDBASEMAN BROUGHT BLACK BASEBALL TO COLORADO."

--JOHN "BUCK" O'NEIL, TEAMMATE

The Ghost was buried in an unmarked grave for many years. In fact, 42 years after his death, Oliver Marcelle's last chapter was finally closed. At 10:30 a.m. on June 1, 1991, members of Riverside's ownership, the Fairmount Cemetery Co., gathered with members of the Erickson Monument Co., the Black American West Museum, and the Denver Zephyrs (the Triple-A inheritors of, in part, Marcelle's Denver baseball legacy) to honor The Ghost one final time. As the culmination of a long effort led by baseball historian and Denver-area resident Jay Sanford, weeks shy of what would have been the legend's 94th birthday, a simple grave marker was unveiled.

Theodore M. "Bubbles" Anderson was a second baseman for the Kansas City Monarchs, the Indianapolis ABS's, and the Birmingham Black Barons. He also played for the local Denver White Elephants. He was buried in Fairmount Cemetery after passing away at the early age of 38, having succumbed to a gastric ulcer. Bubbles also served in the Army in World War II.

The Black Diamond Coal ball club of Boulder, Colorado, gathers for a team portrait. Shown here are, from left to right, (seated in front) Bill Careek's nephew (batboy); (first row) Bud Keeter, Byron "Whizzer" White, Merle Lefferdink, unidentified, and Bill Careek; (second row) unidentified, Landon Persons, Roy Brover, John Earl, Bauldie Moschetti, and Johnnie Ultschi. "Whizzer" White won the Heisman Trophy as college football's best player. He was an all-pro with the Pittsburgh Steelers and Detroit Lions. A Rhodes Scholar, White is the only US Supreme Court justice to hail from Colorado. Moshetti was the founder and manager of the famous Boulder Collegians. Over 70 of Boulder's finest players went on to make names for themselves in the professional ranks.

THE DENVER DREAM

PROGRAM AND SCORE CARD

$2.00

FRIDAY,
SEPT. 30, 1983
MILE HIGH STADIUM

Shown here is the cover of the scorecard and program for the Denver Dream—an all-star game for the ages. The event, a Barry Fey production, brought together an incredible collection of former players in the Mile High City, including several all-time greats. Bob Burris received a phone call that day from the vice president of the United States, George H.W. Bush, politely asking if he could also suit up. The future commander-in-chief and former Yale first baseman played two innings in the field in 1983.

AMERICAN ⚾ LEAGUE

Brooks Robinson

- This man established the standard of excellence for modern day third baseman...
- Set countless fielding records in 23 magnificent seasons with the Baltimore Orioles...
- Eighteen times an All-Star, the American League MVP in 1964 and the World Series MVP in 1970 when he hit .429...
- And now a Hall of Famer...

Moose Skowron

- 14 years in the majors...
- Hit .300 or more five times...
- Hit .388 in a World Series — with 6 home runs and .33 RBI's...
- He appeared in 5 All-Star games and had an All-Star batting average of .429...
- Always an inspirational spirit — and he still has the crew cut...

Mickey Vernon

- Won two batting crowns in his 15 seasons hitting a high of .353 in 1946 with the Washington Senators...
- He holds the American League record for most games played at first base, most assists, and most putouts (19,754)...
- Played in 7 All-Star games...

Hoyt Wilhelm

- Of all the men that have ever pitched a baseball, this man appeared in more games than any other — 1,070, 144 more than CY Young...
- He is also the all-time leader for most wins by a relief pitcher with 123...
- Has a career ERA of 2.52 over 21 years...
- The king of the knuckle ball...

Ted Williams

- Ted was the last player in baseball to bat over .400 for the year...
- He won the MVP award and two Triple Crowns...

AMERICAN ⚾ LEAGUE

The Denver Dream scorecard included details about the participants. This page features Brooks "The Human Vacuum Cleaner" Robinson, Bill "Moose" Skowron, Mickey Vernon, knuckleballer Hoyt Wilhelm, and Ted "The Kid" Williams (also known as "Thumper" and "The Splendid Splinter").

AMERICAN ⚾ LEAGUE

Jose Cardenal

- Acquired by St. Louis in November of 1969 from Cleveland, Jose registered career highs in average (.293) and hits (162) for the Redbirds in 1970.
- He signed his first pro contract with the San Francisco organization in 1961 and made his major league debut with the Giants in 1963.
- In two seasons with the Indians, Jose led the team in stolen bases both years and in 1970 led the team in hits (160), runs (78), triples (7), had the club's longest hitting streak (12 games), and tied a major league record for unassisted double plays by an outfielder (2).

Larry Doby

- Great slugger of the forties and fifties who, 32 years ago broke the color line in the American League when he played his first game for the Cleveland Indians...
- Had five seasons of 100 or more RBI's and eight consecutive seasons of 20 or more home runs...
- From Paterson, New Jersey...

Joe DiMaggio

- In the 40's and 50's — he was everything that our national pastime represents...
- Averaged .325 and 118 RBI's for 13 glorious seasons...
- A three-time American League Batting Champ, a two-time MVP. A Hall of Famer...
- Many rate his 56-game hitting streak in 1941 as baseball's top achievement of all time...
- The "Yankee Clipper"...

Whitey Ford

- Won 236 games in 16 seasons and his .690 winning percentage is the best of any twentieth century pitcher...
- He still holds many World Series records including 10 wins, 94 strikeouts and 33⅔ consecutive scoreless innings...
- The 1961 CY Young Award winner and World Series MVP...
- Hall of Famer...

Bill Freehan

- Spent his entire 15-year career with the Detroit Tigers in the sixties and seventies...
- One of the American League's Premiere backstops during those years, he played on eight All-Star teams and homered off Steve Carlton in the 1969 contest...

The players featured on this page of the Denver Dream scorecard are outfielder Jose Cardenal, baseball pioneer Larry Doby, "Joltin'" Joe DiMaggio, Whitey Ford, and Detroit Tiger Bill Freehan.

AMERICAN ⚾ LEAGUE

118   BARNSTORMERS AND MORE LOCAL LEGENDS

This page of the Denver Dream scorecard highlights outfielder Dale Mitchell, Stan "The Man" Musial, Don "Newk" Newcombe, pitcher Milton Pappas, and Johnny "Pray for Rain" Sain.

Dale Mitchell

- Mitchell began his career in 1946.
- He had the 2nd highest lifetime batting average among active players in '56 and led the American League in fielding in '48 and '49...
- His lifetime batting average is .312.

Photo by George Brace

Stan Musial

- Topped the .300 mark 18 times in a 22-year career and won seven batting titles with the St. Louis Cardinals...
- A three-time National League MVP and an All Star 24 times...
- Had 3,630 lifetime hits and is at or near the top in most every batting category...
- Hall of Famer – "The Man"...

Photo by George Brace

Don Newcombe

- Newcombe, a great Brooklyn Dodgers pitcher, led the Dodgers through several great seasons...
- In 1956 he was the 1st player to win both the Cy Young Award and MVP in the same year...
- In the 1950s he was one of only two players to win more than 25 games in a single season.

Photo by George Brace

Milton (Milt) Pappas

- Pappas passed a milestone in '72, Sept. 18th he pitched his 3,000th inning, becoming one of only 3 active National Leaguers to reach that plateau...
- In 1971, Milt posted a career high of 17 wins (equalled in 1972) and tied for the National League lead with 5 shut-outs...
- Milt ranks 3rd among pitchers in the League in that department with 42 career shut-outs.

Johnny Sain

- Sain was part of the great Boston Braves pitching crew with Warren Spahn.
- He played in the '48 World Series.

Photo by George Brace

Ron Santo

- Starred for the Cubs for 14 seasons, then finished his career with the White Sox...
- Trails only Ernie Banks and Billy Williams with 337 home runs as a Cub...
- Drove in 100 runs four times, including 123 in 1969...
- An eight-time All-Star...

Photo by George Brace

Warren Spahn

- Winningest lefthander in the game's history with 363 victories and was a twenty-game winner 13 times in his 21-year career...
- Still holds National League records for games started and innings pitched...
- The 1957 Cy Young Award winner has pitched 2 no-hitters...
- As tough a competitor as the game has ever known...
- Hall of Famer...

Photo by George Brace

Marv Throneberry

- This Philadelphia Athletics power hitter played in the minor leagues for Denver in '55, '56 and '57.
- He led the league in homers and RBI's during those years...

Photo by George Brace

Billy Williams

- The National League Batting Champion in 1972 when he hit .333 for the Cubs...
- Established a National League record for consecutive games played (1117) broken by Steve Garvey...
- A lifetime .290 hitter in 18 big league seasons, all but 2 with the Chicago Cubs...

Photo by George Brace

Umpires for The Denver Dream are: Shag Crawford, Al Barlick and Tom Gorman.

Special Thanks!

The Denver Dream program could not have been assembled without the assistance of the following baseball collectors and statisticians: Barrie Sullivan, Dave Newbold, Buddy Day, Boney Jackson, H. Wayne Stivers, Mitch Rafal and Ken Arthurs. Baseball Cards (303) 355-4249.

Also appearing tonight is the "Clown Prince of Baseball" Max Patkin.

The Denver Dream announcer... Jack Brickhouse.

Those featured on this page of the Denver Dream scorecard are Ron Santo, Warren Spahn, "Marvelous Marv" Throneberry, Billy Williams, and the "Clown Prince of Baseball," Max Patkin. Also included is Hall of Fame broadcaster Jack Brickhouse.

Orlando Cepeda

• Cepeda was known as "The Baby Bull"...
• He was a great Cardinals third baseman and long ball home run hitter...

GAMES HITS HR R RBI SB AVG.
2124 2351 379 1131 1365 142 .291

Randy Hundley

• Hundley, a valuable Cub catcher, was the first catcher to catch one handed.

GAMES HITS HR R RBI SB AVG.
1061 813 82 308 363 15 .232

This page out of the Denver Dream scorecard highlights "Baby Bull" Orlando Cepeda, catcher Randy Hundley, shortstop Don Kessinger, "Say Hey" Willie Mays, and Willie "Stretch" McCovey.

Don Kessinger

• Six-time All-Star was one of the game's finest shortstops for 13 seasons in Chicago.
• Also managed the White Sox.

GAMES HITS HR R RBI SB AVG.
2077 1931 14 899 527 100 .252

Willie Mays

GAMES HITS HR R RBI SB AVG.
2992 3283 660 2062 1903 338 .302

• This man's remarkable statistics include 3,283 hits, 660 home runs, a lifetime .302 average, two MVP awards and 24 All-Star game appearances...
• Eleven times a Gold Glove corner fielder...
• A Hall of Famer and one of baseball's all-time Greats...
• No one possessed the speed, power and defensive skills of the "Say Hey Kid." #24...

Willie McCovey

• McCovey, a great Giant's 1st baseman, is tied for 8th place on the all time Home Run List with 521 home runs...
• He led the National League in home runs in '63, '68 and '69...
• He was also MVP in '69...

GAMES HITS HR R RBI SB AVG.
2588 2211 521 1229 1555 26 .270

22

Leo Durocher
(Manager)

• After a 17-year major league career as a shortstop in the National League, he had a 24-year managerial career that saw his teams win more than 2,000 games.

Hank Aaron

• Hank is the all-time major league home run hitter with more than 750 home runs...
• An outstanding Brave's player, he is one of only three players in history to have collected over 6000 total bases.

GAMES HITS HR R RBI SB AVG.
3298 3771 755 2174 2297 240 .305

Ernie Banks

• The owner of 512 big league homers and the National League MVP in 1958 and 1959.
• Hit 47 homers in 1958 are the most ever by a shortstop.
• Thirteen times an All-Star.
• A Hall of Famer — Mr. Cub...

GAMES HITS HR R RBI SB AVG.
2528 2583 512 1305 1636 50 .274

Glenn Beckert

• Beckert, a Cub power hitter and second baseman, started playing in 1965. In 1971 he hit .342, was led in National League batting, was named National League All-Star second baseman and was voted to the All-Star team by fans, all in the same year...
• He had a lifetime batting average of .283...

GAMES HITS HR R RBI SB AVG.
1320 1473 22 685 360 49 .283

Lou Brock

• Baseball's all-time stolen base king as he swiped 938 in a 19-year career with the Cubs and Cardinals including 118 in 1974.
• A lifetime .293 hitter who batted .391 in three World Series with the Cardinals...

GAMES HITS HR R RBI SB AVG.
2616 3023 149 1610 900 938 .293

The players featured on this page of the Denver Dream scorecard are "Hammerin'" Hank Aaron, Ernie "Let's Play Two" Banks (also known as "Mr. Cub"), second baseman Glenn Beckert, and stolen-base great Lou Brock.

14

Four-time World Series winner Paul O'Neil played for the Denver Zephyrs before arriving in the major leagues. He played with the Cincinnati Reds and then the New York Yankees.

Barry Larkin, a former Denver Zephyr, played in the major leagues with the Cincinnati Reds. He is now a member of the National Baseball Hall of Fame as well as an analyst on ESPN's *Baseball Tonight*.

Marc Johnson, the legendary baseball coach of the Cherry Creek High School, has amassed over 700 varsity high school baseball victories, an astounding eight state championships, and five state final runner-up finishes since arriving at Cherry Creek in 1972. Coach Johnson led his team to its fifth straight state championship in 1999 and was named National High School Coach of the Decade by *Baseball America*. He was elected into the American Baseball Coaches Association Hall of Fame in January of 2011. Johnson has coached numerous USA baseball teams and has scouted most recently for the Houston Astros and Colorado Rockies organizations. The list of big leaguers hailing from the Cherry Creek program is extensive. In 1995, big leaguers Darnell McDonald, Josh Bard, and Brad Lidge all wore the Bruin red and blue. Others who were guided by Johnson include David Aardsma, John Burke, and Luke Hochevar. An incredibly humble person, Marc Johnson has joined the ranks of great Colorado baseball men and stands as the quintessential symbol of excellence in winning. (Courtesy of Peggy Johnson.)

Pictured are members of the 2010 Denver Browns baseball team. They are, from left to right, (first row) center fielder Tyson Martinez, second baseman Trent Kutler, batboy "Dom-Dom" Granzella, player/manager Matthew Repplinger, and catcher/infielder Dustin Burns; (second row) outfielder/pitcher Justin Hersch, shortstop Dakota Granzella, pitcher Jeremiah Batla, catcher and team captain Chris Campassi, pitcher and team founder Gino Grasso, first baseman Dan Kozloski, and outfielder Evan Martioa. The Browns have established themselves as Denver's top amateur baseball organization, part of the Denver National Adult Baseball Association, boasting a record of 101 wins and 37 loses over six seasons. (Courtesy of Tera Seville.)

The Regis University Raiders celebrate with a team photograph in 2012 after winning the Rocky Mountain Athletic Conference championship for the first time. (Courtesy of Emily Haag.)

Alex Haag holds the 2012 Rocky Mountain Athletic Conference championship trophy. It is the first championship in the long history of Regis University baseball, which dates back to the 19th century. Alex and his family are founders of the Haag Bat Company, which has become the state of Colorado's leading producer of handmade wood-composite baseball bats. (Courtesy of Emily Haag.)

Bruno Konopka (left) was a Denver hero. He is shown here sitting with his skipper, Connie Mack, who has more victories than any manager in the history of the game. Konopka fought in World War II and lost two promising baseball years to the service. He played on men's teams as early as age 15 and had as powerful a swing as any man in Denver.

Visit us at
arcadiapublishing.com

·····································